Lerner SPORTS

KOBE BRYANT

NBA CHAMPION

PERCY LEED

LERNER PUBLICATIONS ◆ MINNEAPOLIS

Copyright © 2021 by Lerner Publishing Group, Inc.

All rights reserved. International copyright secured. No part of this book may be reproduced, stored in a retrieval system, or transmitted in any form or by any means—electronic, mechanical, photocopying, recording, or otherwise—without the prior written permission of Lerner Publishing Group, Inc., except for the inclusion of brief quotations in an acknowledged review.

Lerner Publications Company
An imprint of Lerner Publishing Group, Inc.
241 First Avenue North
Minneapolis, MN 55401 USA

For reading levels and more information, look up this title at www.lernerbooks.com.

Main body text set in Myriad Pro Semibold.
Typeface provided by Adobe.

Designer: Mary Ross **Photo Editor:** Todd Strand
Lerner team: Sue Marquis

Library of Congress Cataloging-in-Publication Data

Names: Leed, Percy, 1968– author.
Title: Kobe Bryant : NBA champion / Percy Leed.
Description: Minneapolis, MN : Lerner Publications, 2021. | Series: Epic sports bios | Includes
  bibliographical references and index. | Audience: Ages 7–11 | Audience: Grades 2–3 | Summary:
  "Kobe Bryant dominated the world of basketball as an 18-time NBA All-Star, a five-time NBA
  champion, and a two-time Olympic gold medalist. This biography details his life and his thrilling
  legacy"— Provided by publisher.
Identifiers: LCCN 2020006272 (print) | LCCN 2020006273 (ebook) | ISBN 9781728419367 (library
  binding) | ISBN 9781728419374 (paperback) | ISBN 9781728419381 (ebook)
Subjects: LCSH: Bryant, Kobe, 1978–2020—Juvenile literature. | Basketball players—United States—
  Biography—Juvenile literature.
Classification: LCC GV884.B794 L44 2021 (print) | LCC GV884.B794 (ebook) | DDC 796.323092 [B]—
  dc23

LC record available at https://lccn.loc.gov/2020006272
LC ebook record available at https://lccn.loc.gov/2020006273

Manufactured in the United States of America
1-49060-49263-4/9/2020

CONTENTS

"SOMETHING SPECIAL" 4

FACTS AT A GLANCE 5

GLOBE-TROTTER 8

FLYING HIGH 12

MOST VALUABLE PLAYER 16

LIFE OF A LEGEND. 21

SIGNIFICANT STATS. 28

GLOSSARY 29

SOURCE NOTES 30

FURTHER INFORMATION 31

INDEX. 32

"SOMETHING SPECIAL"

On January 22, 2006, Kobe Bryant and the Los Angeles Lakers were in big trouble against the Toronto Raptors. When the Lakers stepped onto the court for the second half, Toronto held a 14-point lead. The Raptors quickly grew the lead to 18 points. That's when Bryant began one of the greatest scoring streaks in National Basketball Association (NBA) history.

Kobe Bryant drives down the court against the Raptors in 2006.

FACTS AT A GLANCE

Date of birth: August 23, 1978

Position: forward and guard

League: NBA

Professional highlights: scored 81 points in an NBA game, the second most in league history; won the NBA championship five times; won the NBA Finals Most Valuable Player (MVP) Award twice

Personal highlights: spent seven years in Italy and one year in France as a kid; had four daughters with his wife, Vanessa; won an Oscar for *Dear Basketball*

Bryant hit long three-point shots and midrange jump shots. He spun, twisted, and darted to the basket for layups and slam dunks. No one could stop him. The Lakers outscored the Raptors by 20 points in the third quarter.

Bryant shoots a midrange jump shot.

Bryant was the top scorer in the 2006 season.

In the fourth quarter, Bryant kept shooting, and he rarely missed. Fans went wild as he made basket after basket. The Lakers won the game 122–104.

Bryant racked up 81 points. It was the second most points ever scored in an NBA game. Los Angeles struggled against Toronto before Bryant took over the game. Then, he said, "it turned into something special."

GLOBE-TROTTER

Kobe Bean Bryant was born in Philadelphia, Pennsylvania, on August 23, 1978. His father, Joe Bryant, played forward for the Philadelphia 76ers. He later played for the San Diego Clippers and the Houston Rockets. In 1984, when Kobe was six, Joe began playing for AMG Sebastiani in Rieti, Italy. Kobe, his older sisters, Sharia and Shaya, and their mother, Pamela, followed Joe to Europe.

Joe Bryant played for Philadelphia from 1975–1979.

JELLYBEAN BRYANT

Kobe's middle name, Bean, honors his father's nickname. A teammate on Joe's high school basketball team was amazed by Joe's moves on the court. The teammate said Joe must be made of jelly to move like that. Friends and teammates began calling him Jellybean.

Over the next several years, Joe Bryant played for different teams around Italy. Kobe loved to watch his father play. At halftime and after games, Kobe often went onto the court to shoot baskets with other kids. Joe's teammates noticed Kobe's skills and predicted he would be a great player one day.

As he traveled with his father, Kobe learned to speak Italian. He also learned what it was like to be a pro basketball player. He decided to follow Joe's footsteps and play professional basketball.

Reggio Emilia is located in northern Italy.

By the age of 12, Kobe was already focused on his basketball career. Joe Bryant played for a team in Reggio Emilia, Italy, and Kobe joined a local youth team in the city. Davide Giudici was one of Kobe's teammates. "When he moved to Reggio Emilia and started playing in my team, it was immediately clear he was from another planet, a cut above us all," Giudici said.

Kobe had natural basketball talent, and he worked hard to become the best player he could be. After practice, his teammates usually went home to relax. Kobe went home to shoot baskets with the hoop in his yard.

After seven years in Italy and one year in France, Kobe and his family returned to Philadelphia. Joe's basketball career was finished, but Kobe's was about to take off. In 1992, he enrolled at Lower Merion High School and quickly became a basketball sensation.

Kobe talks to reporters at Lower Merion High School.

FLYING HIGH

As a freshman in 1992, Kobe joined Merion's varsity basketball team. He worked hard as one of the youngest players on the team, but they didn't have much success. Merion finished the season with a 4–20 record.

As they gained experience together, Kobe and his teammates began to play better. Kobe led the way. In 1994, he had more than 30 points and 10 rebounds per game.

Kobe dunks during a Merion practice.

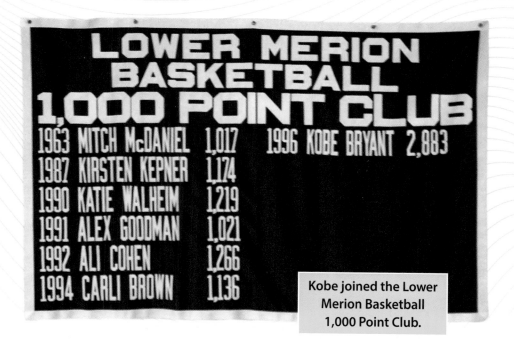

LOWER MERION BASKETBALL 1,000 POINT CLUB

1963	MITCH McDANIEL	1,017
1987	KIRSTEN KEPNER	1,174
1990	KATIE WALHEIM	1,219
1991	ALEX GOODMAN	1,021
1992	ALI COHEN	1,266
1994	CARLI BROWN	1,136
1996	KOBE BRYANT	2,883

Kobe joined the Lower Merion Basketball 1,000 Point Club.

The next season, he was even better. Kobe led Merion to their first state championship since 1943. He won several national player of the year awards.

Kobe finished his high school career with 2,883 points. His scoring set a new state record. After the team's poor performance in 1992, Kobe led Merion to an incredible 77–13 record over the next three seasons. He was ready for bigger challenges.

Almost all NBA players take the same path to the league. They star on a high school team, play at least one year of college basketball, and then enter the NBA Draft.

Kobe holds up his jersey after being traded to the Lakers.

In 1995, Kevin Garnett went straight from high school to the NBA. He became the first high school player drafted in 20 years.

Kobe wanted to do the same. The 1996 NBA Draft took place in New Jersey on June 26. The Charlotte Hornets chose Kobe with the 13th overall pick and then traded him to the Lakers. At 17 years old, Kobe still wasn't a legal adult. His parents signed the contract to finalize his deal with Los Angeles.

As a rookie in 1996–1997, Kobe wasn't usually a starter. When a game began, he was on the bench, watching his teammates. But as the game wore on, Kobe got into the action. In just over 15 minutes, he averaged almost eight points.

In February 1997, Kobe won the NBA's Slam Dunk Contest. He soared through the air for a series of amazing dunks. In one move, he jumped, passed the ball between his legs, and then slammed it through the hoop. The crowd roared as he celebrated on the court. In the years to come, Kobe would continue to give Lakers fans many reasons to cheer.

YOUNG STAR

On November 3, 1996, Kobe played against the Minnesota Timberwolves in his first NBA game. In just over six minutes, he missed a shot, grabbed a rebound, and blocked a shot on defense. The Lakers won, 91–85, and Kobe became the youngest person to ever play in an NBA game.

MOST VALUABLE PLAYER

In his third NBA season, Bryant became a full-time starter. He scored almost 20 points per game. Los Angeles reached the playoffs and defeated the Houston Rockets in the first round. But in the second round, the San Antonio Spurs beat Los Angeles in four straight games.

Bryant drives past Kevin Garnett in 1999.

Bryant and Phil Jackson
discuss strategy
during a game.

The Lakers needed a change and hired Phil Jackson as head coach. Jackson had led Michael Jordan and the Chicago Bulls to six NBA championships in eight years.

With Jackson in charge, the Lakers became the best team in the NBA. Bryant and center Shaquille O'Neal were unstoppable together. Bryant played tough defense and could make shots from anywhere. O'Neal's huge size helped him control the area near the basket at both ends of the court.

The Lakers finished the 1999–2000 season with the best record in the NBA. Then they stormed through the playoffs and beat the Indiana Pacers in the NBA Finals.

O'Neal won the Finals MVP Award. But Bryant was just as important to the team's success. Jerry Buss, then the Lakers owner, said what many Los Angeles fans were thinking, "They're the two best players in basketball."

Bryant soars over defenders to the basket.

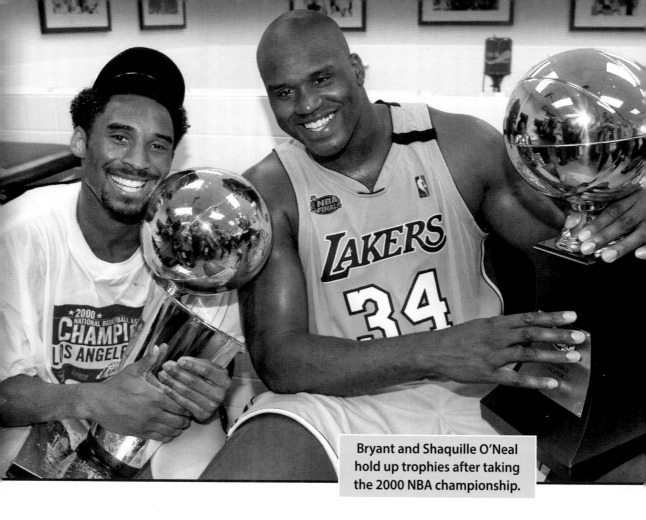

Bryant and Shaquille O'Neal hold up trophies after taking the 2000 NBA championship.

Buss was right. Bryant and O'Neal proved it in 2000–2001 and again in 2001–2002 by winning two more championships. O'Neal was named Finals MVP three years in a row.

After the 2003–2004 season, O'Neal left Los Angeles and joined the Miami Heat. Without their big center, the Lakers struggled. They missed the playoffs in 2004–2005. The next two seasons, they lost early in the playoffs.

Bryant worked harder than ever. He ran, lifted weights, and took hundreds of practice shots a day. In the 2007–2008 playoffs, Bryant led the league in scoring and helped the Lakers make the Finals. They lost to the Boston Celtics in six games.

The Lakers reached the Finals again in 2009, and this time, Bryant wouldn't let his team lose. They topped the Orlando Magic in five games, and Bryant won the Finals MVP Award. Los Angeles won back-to-back titles by beating the Celtics in 2010. "I wanted it so, so bad," Bryant said. His scoring, leadership, and desire to win helped him become the Finals MVP again.

OLYMPIC CHAMP

In 2008, Bryant and Team USA won the men's basketball gold medal at the Olympic Games in Beijing, China. As usual, one championship wasn't enough for Bryant. Four years later, he helped the United States win gold at the 2012 Olympic Games in London, England.

LIFE OF A LEGEND

With five championships, Bryant was one of the most successful players in NBA history. In December 2014, he proved it again. He entered a game against the Timberwolves with 32,284 career points. In the third quarter, he passed Michael Jordan for third place on the NBA's all-time scoring list.

Bryant averaged 22.3 points per game in the 2014–2015 season.

Bryant smiles while announcing his retirement in 2015.

The 2015–2016 season was Bryant's 20th in the NBA. He had nothing left to prove, and he was tired from years of hard work. In November 2015, he announced he would retire after the season.

Bryant ended his career like a true scoring champion. In April 2016, the Lakers faced the Utah Jazz in Los Angeles.

Fans, celebrities, and reporters packed the arena for Bryant's final game. He scored 60 points in a 101–96 victory.

After retiring, Bryant spent more time with his wife, Vanessa Bryant, raising their four daughters: Natalia, Gianna, Bianka, and Capri. He also had more time to give back to the community. The Kobe and Vanessa Bryant Family Foundation provides money to young people for education and sports programs.

In 2017, the Lakers retired Bryant's jersey numbers. No other Lakers players will ever wear 8 and 24 again.

Bryant works with kids to make care packages.

Bryant also worked with groups such as the Make-A-Wish Foundation, which grants wishes to children with life-threatening illnesses. Many kids wanted to meet their Lakers basketball hero. More than 100 times, Bryant met with kids and made their dreams come true.

In 2018, Bryant won another prize. With a former Disney animator, he created a short film called *Dear Basketball*. The movie was based on a poem Bryant wrote announcing his retirement. It won an Academy Award for Best Short Film (Animated).

Bryant holds up his Academy Award for *Dear Basketball*.

Fans gather at the Lakers's stadium, Staples Center, to honor Bryant.

Bryant was living a full life after basketball. On January 26, 2020, he flew in a helicopter to attend Gianna's basketball game. The aircraft crashed, killing Bryant, his daughter, and seven others aboard.

People around the world were shocked. Fans, players, and politicians all expressed grief at the news. Thousands of people went to Staples Center. They left flowers, basketballs, and other items to honor Bryant. Many vowed to keep his memory alive. The five-time champion won't be forgotten, on or off the court.

Bryant and Gianna shared a love of basketball.

SIGNIFICANT STATS

Voted to play in 18 NBA All-Star Games

Voted NBA All-Star Game MVP four times

Won the NBA MVP Award for the 2007–2008 season

Won the NBA Finals MVP Award twice

Led the NBA in scoring twice

Won the NBA championship five times

Won two Olympic gold medals for men's basketball

GLOSSARY

animator: an artist involved in creating animated cartoons

center: a player who usually stays close to the basket and the middle of the court

draft: when teams take turns choosing new players

forward: a basketball position that plays similar to a center with more movement around the court

jump shot: a shot taken after jumping off the court

layup: a one-handed shot near the basket

rebound: the act of grabbing and controlling the ball after a missed shot

slam dunk: a shot made by jumping high into the air and throwing the ball down through the basket

starter: one of the players on the court when a game begins

varsity: the top team at a school

SOURCE NOTES

7   NBA.com staff, "Top Moments: Kobe Bryant Drops 81 Points on Raptors in '06," NBA. com, accessed January 31, 2020, https://www .nba.com/history/top-moments/2006-kobe-bryant-81-points.

10   Claudio Lavanga, "A View of Kobe Bryant from His Childhood Home in Italy," NBC News, January 27, 2020, https://www.nbcnews.com /news/world/view-kobe-bryant-his-childhood-home-italy-n1123716.

18   Tim Kawakami, "With Shaq and Kobe in the Starring Roles, Lakers Win First Championship in a Dozen Years," *Los Angeles Times*, June 20, 2000, https://www.latimes.com/archives/la-xpm-2000-jun-20-sp -42872-story.html.

20   Associated Press, "NBA Finals MVP: Kobe Bryant Says This Championship Is the 'Sweetest,'" *Christian Science Monitor*, June 18, 2010, https://www.csmonitor.com/From-the-news-wires/2010/0618 /NBA-Finals-MVP-Kobe-Bryant-says-this-championship-is-the -sweetest.

FURTHER INFORMATION

Basketball Reference: Kobe Bryant
https://www.basketball-reference.com/players/b/bryanko01.html

Kidzworld: Kobe Bryant
https://www.kidzworld.com/article/3690-kobe-bryant-biography

Monson, James. *Behind the Scenes Basketball*. Minneapolis: Lerner Publications, 2020.

The Players' Tribute: "Dear Basketball"
https://www.theplayerstribune.com/en-us/articles/dear-basketball

Scheff, Matt. *NBA and WNBA Finals*. Minneapolis: Lerner Publications, 2021.

Uhl, Xina M. *Kobe Bryant*. New York: Rosen, 2019.

INDEX

Bryant, Gianna, 23, 26

Bryant, Joe, 8–11

Chicago Bulls, 17

Dear Basketball, 5, 25

Jackson, Phil, 17

Los Angeles Lakers, 4, 6–7, 14–20, 22, 24

Lower Merion High School, 11–13

Olympic Games, 20

O'Neal, Shaquille, 17–19

Reggio Emilia, Italy, 10

PHOTO ACKNOWLEDGMENTS

Image credits: AP Photo/Matt A. Brown, pp. 4, 6, 7; Pongnathee Kluaythong/EyeEm/Getty Images, pp. 5, 28; Focus on Sport/Getty Images, p. 8; Giuliani Claudio//Wikimedia Commons (CC BY-SA 4.0), p. 10; AP Photo/Rusty Kennedy, pp. 11, 12; Gina Ferazzi/Los Angeles Times/Getty Images, p. 13; Steve Grayson/WireImage/Getty Images, p. 14; CRAIG LASSIG/AFP/Getty Images, p. 16; Jonathan Ferrey/Getty Images, p. 17; JOHN G. MABANGLO/AFP/Getty Images, p. 18; AFP/Getty Images, p. 19; Hannah Foslien/Getty Images, p. 21; Kevork Djansezian/Getty Images, p. 22; Allen Berezovsky/Getty Images, p. 23; Chip Somodevilla/Getty Images, p. 24; Ian West - PA Images/Getty Images, p. 25; APU GOMES/AFP/Getty Images, p. 26; Ethan Miller/Getty Images, p. 27. Design element throughout: saicle/iStock/Getty Images.

Cover: Mike Ehrmann/Getty Images; Kevork Djansezian/Getty Images (background).